Reigning
Cats & Dogs

Reigning Cats & Dogs

A RHYMES WITH ORANGE tribute to those who shed

by Hilary B. Price

**Andrews McMeel
Publishing**

Kansas City

Rhymes with Orange is syndicated internationally by King Features Syndicate, Inc. For information, write King Features Syndicate, Inc., 888 Seventh Avenue, New York, NY 10019.

03 04 05 06 07 WKT 10 9 8 7 6 5 4 3

ISBN: 0-7407-3306-0

Library of Congress Control Number: 2002111891

——— **ATTENTION: SCHOOLS AND BUSINESSES** ———

Andrews McMeel books are available at quantity discounts with bulk purchase for educational, business, or sales promotional use. For information, please write to: Special Sales Department, Andrews McMeel Publishing, 4520 Main Street, Kansas City, Missouri 64111.

For Kerry

Introduction

Every day I open the garage, get out my bicycle, hook my dog onto her leash, and the two of us set out to my studio a mile away. She has her own chair there, with a view of the front door so she can bark at the UPS guy without actually getting up.

Bringing my dog to work is one of my favorite things about having this job. One of my other favorite things is the e-mail I get from readers offering their stories and support. Invariably, they include a dog or cat story, many of which have inspired the cartoons to follow.

It's been confirmed many times over that the people who enjoy *Rhymes With Orange* are smart, witty, and incredibly good-looking. I'm lucky to have you as my readers.

Enjoy the book.

Hilary B. Price

October, 2002

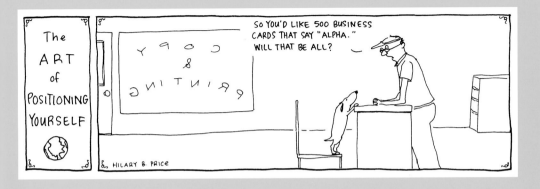

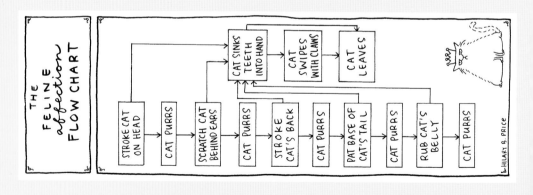

THE ANNUAL GALA

I'd like to thank the Acatemy...

AND THIS YEAR'S WINNER FOR THE BEST PERFORMANCE OF "NO, NO, THE OTHER PERSON WHO LIVES HERE HAS DEFINITELY NOT FED ME WET FOOD YET TODAY" GOES TO...

HILARY B. PRICE

FELINE CHEMISTRY

CATS ARE PARTICULARY SENSITIVE TO THE LAWS OF THERMODYNAMICS:

With heat, we expand.

PUT A CAT ON A WARM BED WITH TWO PEOPLE AND BEHOLD - IT TAKES UP ALL OF THE ROOM.

Honey? Honey?!

HILARY B. PRICE   "Thanks Matt"

OWNERS BEWARE: GET A LARGER MATTRESS OR FACE THE CONSEQUENCES...

I woke up today with my head on the bedside table.

18

19

24

THE SOCIALLY ACCEPTABLE LIMITS

THE THREE-SECOND RULE:
THE TIME PEOPLE ALLOW FOR FOOD TO BE ON THE GROUND AND STILL BE PICKED UP AND EATEN.

I'll just blow on it

THE THREE-WEEK RULE:
THE SAME RULE, BUT FOR DOGS.

chomp chomp chomp

A sand-encrusted, dried-up hotdog! It's my lucky day!

HILARY B. PRICE

THE WARNING

Are we CLEAR, Brewster?

THE LAST TIME I TIPPED OVER THE GARBAGE, SHE SPELLED IT OUT. SHE SAID, "REMEMBER-- THERE'S ONLY A *fine line* BETWEEN 'pet' AND 'pelt.'"

HILARY "Thanks S. Mikula" PRICE

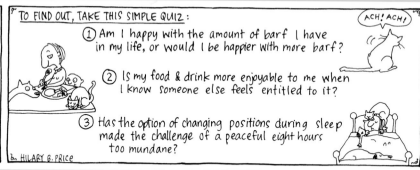

ARE **YOU** READY for a DOG, CAT or CHILD?

TO FIND OUT, TAKE THIS SIMPLE QUIZ:

1. Am I happy with the amount of barf I have in my life, or would I be happier with more barf?

2. Is my food & drink more enjoyable to me when I know someone else feels entitled to it?

3. Has the option of changing positions during sleep made the challenge of a peaceful eight hours too mundane?

ACH! ACH!

— HILARY B. PRICE

FROM THE HEART ♡

I WANT SOMETHING THAT SHOWS HOW MUCH I REALLY LOVE HER.

— HILARY B. PRICE

26

27

THE FLATLANDS

I WOULD LIKE TO THINK THAT WAS A TUMBLEWEED.

WE KNOW IT'S CAT HAIR.

A *Rhymes With Orange*

TRUE FELINE FACTOID

IT'S BELIEVED THAT CATS DON'T RECOGNIZE PEOPLE BY THEIR FACES, BUT INSTEAD BY THE WAY THEY MOVE.

WHAT DOES YOUR CAT SEE IN YOU?

PRINCESS!

QUASIMODO! PIGEON TOES! YOU'RE BACK!

34

DEALING WITH THE VETERINARIAN'S BILL

Having a sick pet is hard both emotionally and financially.

$100 for the lab tests, $25 for the antibiotic, $300 for the surgery and $50 for the teeth-cleaning we did while he was under.

Sitting quietly with your pet and thinking about the priceless companionship he or she offers is a good way to deal with the expense.

Calculating how much your pet is costing per pound is not.

HILARY B. PRICE

38

THE SOCIAL NICETIES

mmpf!

MY GIVEN NAME IS "BUTT-IN-YOUR-FACE," BUT FOR COMPANY THEY'VE SHORTENED IT TO "BUTTON."

HILARY "Thanks KC Remington" Price

ANIMAL CAMOUFLAGE TECHNIQUES wild vs. domestic

Wild

ANIMALS THRIVE BY HAVING THEIR APPEARANCE MIMIC THEIR ENVIRONMENT.

Domestic

WHERE'S THE CAT? shed shed shed

NO, WHERE'S THE COUCH?

HILARY B. PRICE

ANIMALS THRIVE BY HAVING THEIR ENVIRONMENT MIMIC THEIR APPEARANCE.

BACK TO TWO

HOW ABOUT A "W-A-L-K?"

STANLEY, THE DOG'S GONE. THE KIDS ARE GROWN. FOR THE LOVE OF PETE, STOP SPELLING AT ME.

HILARY B. PRICE

THE SURPRISE

Cracker Jacks

COME SPRING, PEOPLE PUT AWAY THEIR HEAVY COATS AND PULL ON THEIR LIGHT JACKETS.

HILARY B. PRICE

FOR SOME, THERE'S THE THRILL OF FINDING FORGOTTEN MONEY STASHED IN A FRONT POCKET.

Hey! Five bucks!

...IT'S NEVER AS EXCITING FOR DOG OWNERS.

Two liver snaps and a plastic bag?

THE ART of BOTHERING THE DOG

As your dog naps quietly, play with the pads of her feet. Gently stick your fingers between her toes until she twitches them away. Continue until she gets up and naps elsewhere.

Put on some music. Pick up your dog's front legs and have him dance with you. Continue dancing until he pulls away and exits the room.

As your dog quietly minds her own business, place a towel over her head and watch her try to get it off. Then put sunglasses or antlers (depending on the season) on her and try to take pictures.

NOTE: No dogs were actually bothered in the making of this comic strip.   HILARY B. PRICE

44

46

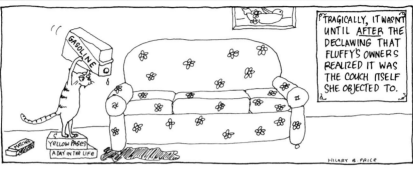

47

49

THE NAME GAME

Panel 1:

WHEN NAMING PETS, PEOPLE EITHER GO SCHMALTZY OR RIDICULOUS:

I'm Bunny-Wunny.

Widget here!

Call me Thoreau Emerson.

Panel 2:

WE DO THIS BECAUSE WE CAN GET AWAY WITH IT-- OUR PETS WON'T BLAME US FOR RUINING THEIR LIVES WITH A STUPID NAME.

How could you do this to me?

Do what, Scratchy?

HILARY B. PRICE

Panel 3:

IT'S REALLY ONLY ONCE A YEAR OUR CHOICE COMES UNDER SCRUTINY:

Creamsicle Sipowitz? The vet's ready for you.

A CAT'S MAP OF THE BED

Invisible to the naked eye...

NIGHT TIME SLEEPING REGION
HEAVING SPOT
YOGA & STRETCHING STUDIO
GROOMING
LAUNCH PAD TO THE DRESSER
PARLOUR
SALON
FOOT ATTACK ZONE
MEDITATION AREA
NAPPING QUARTERS

HILARY B. PRICE

POST VET

I HATE THESE CONES! COULD THERE BE ANYTHING MORE EMBARRASSING?

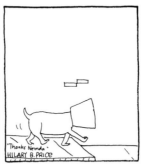

"Thanks Nevada"
HILARY B. PRICE

DOG DREAMS

IT WAS THE WEIRDEST DREAM... WE WERE ROLLING IN POOP IN YOUR BACKYARD, BUT IT WASN'T REALLY YOUR BACKYARD, IT WAS SOMEONE ELSE'S...

HILARY B. PRICE

WITH THIS STICK,
PEPPER KNEW SHE'D
BE THE ENVY OF THE
OTHER DOGS.

HILARY B. PRICE

59

LIFE SKILLS 101

As children, many of us insisted that all of our stuffed animals sleep on the bed, despite the little room it left for us...

Few knew what preparation this might be for later life.

Are any of you going to move?

We just got comfortable.

HILARY B. PRICE

FELINE INSOMNIA

The first few hours I tossed and turned, but the next twenty-six went okay.

HILARY B. PRICE

61

Fred knew he was destined for something else.

SELF - IMPROVEMENT

THE GENES

FETCH!

THE SHELTER SAID SHE WAS PART RETRIEVER.

HILARY B. PRICE   "Thanks Helen"

TURNS OUT IT'S THE PART THAT GOES AFTER THE STICK, NOT THE PART THAT BRINGS IT BACK.

THE HUNT

You have a beautiful dog!

WHAT A DISAPPOINTMENT-- I THOUGHT HE SAID, "LETS GO TO THE PARK AND CHASE SQUIRRELS," NOT "GIRLS."

HILARY B. PRICE

69

WINTER CHILL

72

THE RELAY

ZOOM

THEN I PASS THE BATON TO YOU, AND YOU HIT THAT LAST STRETCH LIKE IT'S A DARK HALLWAY AT TWO IN THE MORNING.

HILARY B. PRICE

DESCRIBE UTOPIA

Z.

A PLACE WHERE ALL PEOPLE ARE TREATED WITH KINDNESS & RESPECT.

A PLACE WHERE THE ENVIRONMENT IS CHERISHED & TAKEN CARE OF.

A PLACE WHERE EVERYONE HAS ENOUGH FOOD.

A NICE BASKET OF CLEAN LAUNDRY.

HILARY B. PRICE

80

Strip 1:

THE NEXT PHASE

Yellow Jacket Pit Hound

WE USED TO BREED DOGS WITH A SPECIFIC PURPOSE IN MIND.

Terriers to catch rats...

Collies to herd sheep...

Golden Retrievers to help us feel intellectually superior...

BUT MOST OF THESE SKILLS ARE NO LONGER NEEDED. SO WHY DON'T WE BREED FOR SKILLS WE DO NEED?

I need a dog that can catch a bee in a cup and release it outside.

Start him out with moths. He'll be ready for bees in 3 weeks.

HILARY B. PRICE

"Thanks Rachel"

Strip 2:

THUNDER SURVIVAL TACTICS

BOOM

HILARY B. PRICE

83

85

THE ART of FELINE DISCIPLINE

THE GROOMING SESSIONS